JESUS
Teaches His Disciples

Contemporary Bible Series
JESUS Teaches His Disciples

Retold by Joy Melissa Jensen

Published by Scandinavia Publishing House 2009
Drejervej 15,3   DK-2400 Copenhagen NV, Denmark
E-mail: info@sph.as
Web: www.sph.as

Text copyright © Scandinavia Publishing House
Illustrations copyright © Gustavo Mazali
Design by Ben Alex
Printed in China
ISBN 978 87 7247 507 3

JESUS
Teaches His Disciples
Retold for Children

by Joy Melissa Jensen

scandinavia

Contents

Mary and Martha
Luke 10:38-42

Jesus was traveling with his disciples. They were weary and tired from the journey. When they came to the village of Bethany, they stopped to rest.

Martha and Mary were two sisters who lived in Bethany. They welcomed Jesus and his disciples to stay in their home. Martha had heard about Jesus, and she knew he was a special guest. She began to worry and fuss about the way her house looked.

"What if Jesus thought it looked shabby," she worried. So Martha rushed around, dusting and sweeping and cooking and cleaning.

Martha's sister had also heard of Jesus. She was so excited to see him that she sat right down on the floor in front of him. As Jesus spoke, Mary listened to every word he said. Martha was annoyed by this. "I'm doing all the work," she told Jesus. "Mary is doing none. Don't you think that's unfair?"

Jesus answered, "Martha, you are so upset! But only one thing is necessary. Mary has chosen what is best. She has chosen to listen to my words."

4

The Farmer's Seeds

Mark 4:1-20

While Jesus was teaching by the Sea of Galilee, a big crowd gathered who had come to hear him speak. There were so many people that Jesus had to teach from a boat on the lake while the crowd stood on the shore. He told them this story, saying,

"A farmer went out to scatter his seeds. Some seeds fell between the rocks. They sprouted, but died quickly because there was not enough deep soil to grow strong roots. Some seeds fell among the thorn bushes. These were choked by the prickles. But a few of the farmer's seeds fell on good ground. These seeds

turned into a great harvest, ten times the size of what had been planted.

"It is the same with God's people!" Jesus said. "Some do not hear what I say, and the message does not grow within them. But the ones who hear my words will be rewarded."

Then a disciple called out, "Jesus, why do you always tell stories?"

So Jesus explained, "Many people hear, but they don't really hear. Many people see, but they don't really see. I tell stories so that your eyes, ears and hearts will understand God's message!"

7

Wheat and Weeds

Matthew 13:24-30, 36-39

Jesus told this story next. He said, "Once, a farmer scattered his seeds in a field. After he left, an enemy came and scattered weeds in that same field. The plants began to grow, and the weed grew right along with the plants. The servants of the farmer ran to him and said, 'Sir, why are there weeds growing among your grain?' The farmer replied, 'An enemy must have done this. Leave the weeds alone until harvest time. Otherwise you may pull up the wheat when you are trying to pull out the

weeds. When the time is right, we will separate the two and throw the weeds away.'

Jesus explained, "The farmer's good seeds are like the people who hear my message and take it to heart," Jesus said, "But the weeds are like the people who do not listen. Someday God will bring judgment to his people. God will separate them, just like the farmer separated the weeds from his wheat."

Seed and Yeast

Mark 4:26-29; Matthew 13:31-34

"Even while the farmer is asleep," Jesus said, "the seeds he scattered keep growing from the soil that nurtures them. Take a look at a mustard seed! It's the smallest of the seeds. But when it is fully grown it is huge. Even the birds build nests in its big leafy branches! It is the same with the littlest of God's children.

They grow mighty in God's love. Everyone around them benefits from their faith."

"Now think of a woman making bread," Jesus continued. "How would the dough turn into bread without the yeast that makes it rise? The yeast is important even though it is small. The Kingdom of Heaven, too, depends on the smallest of God's children to make it grow!"

The Greatest in Heaven

Matthew 18:1-14

Then the disciples asked Jesus, "Who will be the greatest in God's kingdom?" Jesus smiled. He looked around and saw a child peeking out from behind the people in the crowd. Then he called the child over and pulled him gently into his arms.

"I promise you this," said Jesus to the disciples, "If you don't change and become like this child, you will never get into the kingdom of heaven. A child accepts God with a pure and humble heart. If you do this, you will be the greatest in God's kingdom. When you welcome one of these children, you welcome me. Don't be cruel to any of these little ones! Their angels are with my God in heaven."

"Now let me ask you this," Jesus said. "What would you do if you had a hundred sheep and one was lost? Wouldn't you leave the others to find the lost one? I am sure that finding the one lost sheep would make you happier than having all the rest that were not lost. That is how it is with my Father in heaven. He doesn't want any of these little ones to be lost."

Let the Children Come to Me

Mark 10:13-16

Many parents brought their children to Jesus hoping he would bless them. The children crowded around Jesus and began to play with him. But Jesus' disciples tried to keep them from coming near Jesus.

"Step back," they instructed the children. "Jesus doesn't want to be bothered."

But Jesus cried out, "Let the children come to me! Don't stop them. These children belong to the kingdom of God. None of you can enter God's kingdom unless you accept it the way a child does. Learn from them!"

Then Jesus opened his arms and the little children ran giggling and smiling, wrapping their arms around Jesus' neck. Jesus placed his hands on them and blessed each one. He told them, "Every one of you is welcome into my Father's kingdom."

The Good Shepherd

John 10:11-18

Jesus said, "I am the good shepherd and you are my flock. The shepherd will give up his life for his sheep. But hired workers don't own the sheep, so they do not care about them. When a wolf comes, they run off and leave the sheep to be taken and eaten. But each little sheep is important to me. If one is lost, I will search high and low until that sheep is found! I love my

16

sheep, and they love me just as the Father loves me, and I love the Father. I bring all my sheep together into one flock and watch over them. I will gladly give up my life for my sheep. No one takes my life from me. I give it up willingly! I have the power to give up my life and the power to receive it back again just as my Father commanded me to do."

The Lost Sheep
and the Lost Coin

Luke 15:1-10

Jesus was talking and eating with a small group of people when some sinners came up and began to listen to his words. Jesus welcomed them. But his disciples and some of the Pharisees began to point and stare. "Look at Jesus," they scowled. "He is eating with a bunch of sinners!" Jesus heard them say these things. He turned and faced them.

"Imagine," Jesus said, "that you are a shepherd, and you have lost one of your sheep. Won't you leave the ninety-nine others behind and find the lost one?

When you find the sheep, you will be so glad that you will carry it home on your shoulders. Then you will say to your friends, 'Let's celebrate! I've found the one that was lost.'"

"There is more happiness for my Father in heaven if one sinner turns to God than ninety-nine good people who did not need to. And what about a woman who loses one coin in a stack of ten coins? Won't she light a lamp, sweep the floor, and look carefully until she has found it? My Father in heaven will celebrate when one of these sinners who sit with me turn to him."

The Two Sons

Luke 15:11-19

Jesus told a story:

A man had two sons. He loved them both and wanted to see them do well. He planned to divide his property and money between them. The younger son said, "Father, please give me my share. I want to go out in the world and become successful."

He took off and traveled to a faraway country. He spent all his money on silly things. Before he knew it, he reached into his pocket, and there was not one coin left. Desperate for money, the younger son got a job working for a pig farmer. His clothes turned ragged and dirty. His stomach was always growling with hunger. He would've been happy to eat the slop from the trough of the pigs. But at last he thought, "This is foolish! My father treats his servants better than this! I will go to him and ask his forgiveness. Perhaps he will accept me, and I will offer to work for him."

So the son started on the long journey home again back to his father's house.

The Youngest Son Returns

Luke 15:20-32

Jesus continued telling the story:

The father spotted his youngest son walking toward home. He ran out to meet him and showered him in hugs and kisses. He called to his servants, "Bring out our finest clothes! Prepare a big feast! Put a shiny ring on my son's finger! He was lost, and now he is found!" The older son was out in the field working. He ran back to the house to see what had happened.

"What's going on?" he asked.

"Your brother is back!" the servants replied.

The older brother became angry. He ran to his father and said, "I have been working like a slave for you. I have obeyed you. I have always done everything you asked me to. But my brother runs away, spends all your money and disobeys you. Why are you treating him like a prince?" His father answered, "Son, you always did right and obeyed me. You were never lost, but your brother was lost. Be happy and celebrate with me. He has come back to us!"

The Two Prayers

Luke 18:9-14

One day, Jesus came upon some people who were acting proud and self-righteous. He walked over to them and told them this story:

Two men went into a temple to pray. One was a Pharisee and the other was a tax collector. The Pharisee prayed, "Thank you for making me good. I am not greedy or dishonest. I am faithful in marriage, and I have always given part of my money to you." But the tax collector stayed in the far corner of the temple. He did not think he was good enough to even look up toward heaven. He hung his head and prayed, "God, have pity on me! I am such a sinner."

"Whom do you think God was pleased with more?" Jesus asked. "The man who bragged about how good he was or the man who admitted to his sins? Remember, if you hold yourself high above others, you will be put down. But if you are humble and admit your sins, you will be honored."

25

Jesus Teaches an Important Lesson

John 8:1-11

Early one morning Jesus went to the temple where he usually went to teach. People were crowding around to hear his lesson. Suddenly a group of angry men burst through the door. They were holding a woman roughly by the arm. "Teacher!" they shouted. "This woman has been caught sleeping with a man who was not her husband. This woman should be stoned for her sins! What do you say?" They asked Jesus this question because they wanted to test him. Would he say yes or no? But Jesus said neither. Instead he looked around at the crowd that had gathered and said, "Let the person who has never sinned throw the first stone!" The men were speechless. They looked around at one another but no one volunteered to throw the

first stone because they all had sinned. One by one the men walked away until only Jesus and the woman were left. "Isn't there anyone left to accuse you?" Jesus asked the woman. The woman shook her head. "Then I will not accuse you either," Jesus said. "You are forgiven, but sin no more!"

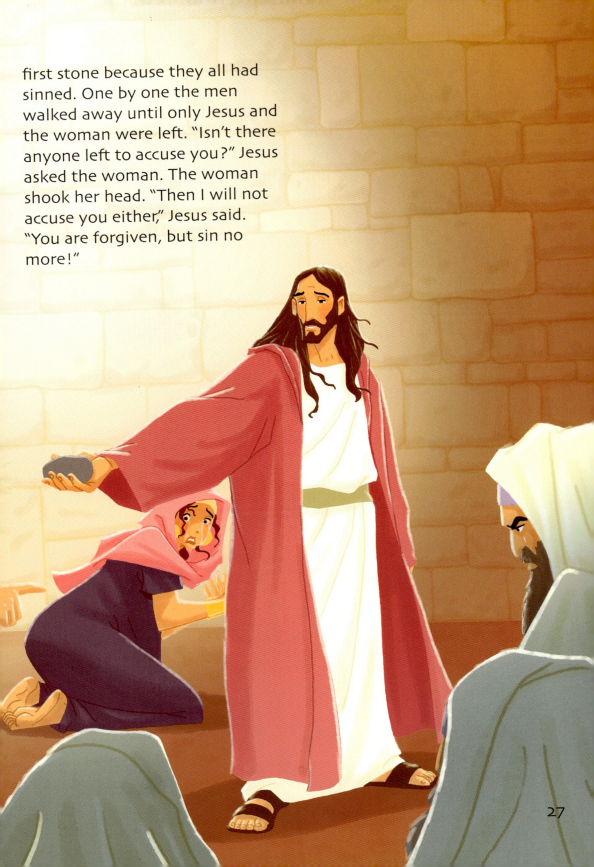

A Woman Washes Jesus' Feet

Luke 7:36-40

A Pharisee named Simon invited Jesus to have dinner with him. There was a woman who had heard that Jesus was at Simon's house. She was a sinner, and everyone in the village looked down on her. The woman loved Jesus. She went to Simon's house and brought an expensive bottle of perfume. When the woman saw Jesus, she fell down on the floor near his feet, and she began to cry tears of love. Her tears fell on Jesus' feet and she began to wash and dry them with her hair. Next the woman poured her expensive perfume on Jesus' feet; then she covered them with her kisses.

Simon had been watching all of this. He felt confused and angry. "If Jesus were really a prophet of God," Simon thought, "he would know what kind of a sinner this woman was."

Jesus knew what Simon was thinking. He said, "Simon, I'd like to tell you a story."

29

A Sinner's Love

Luke 7:41-50

Jesus told this story to Simon:

Two people owed money to a moneylender. One of them owed five hundred silver coins, and the other owed fifty silver coins. The moneylender was a kind man and decided that neither of them had to pay the money back. One of the men simply thanked the moneylender and went about his way. The other man jumped for joy, bowing and kissing the ground at the moneylender's feet.

"Which one of the men was more grateful to the moneylender?" Jesus asked Simon.

"The man that owed five hundred silver coins," Simon answered, "because he owed so much more."

Jesus smiled and said, "Now Simon, have you noticed this woman? From the moment I arrived she has been with me, washing and kissing my feet. She has even poured expensive perfume on them! You did not do any of these things. She is like the one who owed five hundred silver coins and did not have to pay any of them back. All of her many sins are forgiven. That is why she shows great love!" Then Jesus turned to the woman and said, "Your sins are forgiven. Because of your faith you are saved."

30

31

The Rich Offering of a Poor Widow

Mark 12:41-44

Jesus was sitting in the temple near the offering box. He was watching people put in their money gifts to God. The rich people put in handfuls of money. The coins clinked and clanked as they fell into the box. The rich people looked proud that they could give so much. Then an old widow went up to the box. She put in the only two coins she had.

Jesus told his disciples to gather around. Then he said, "This poor widow has put in more than all the others." The disciples shook their heads and said, "She has only put in a couple of coins!"

Jesus nodded. Then he said, "You see, the many coins of the rich do not mean much. They are like loose change in their pockets. But the few coins of the poor are as valuable as gold. They have given the little bit they have up to God."

33

Treasures in Heaven

Matthew 6:19-30

Jesus was speaking to a large crowd that had gathered outside one morning.

He said, "All the things you have here on earth are of little worth. A moth can come and chew your clothes. Rust can ruin your favorite cups and plates.

Thieves can come and steal your money. Don't store up these things that can be taken from you. Treasures in heaven cannot be taken from you. Put your heart in God alone! You cannot love riches and God at the same time. Have faith that God will take care of you. He will give you everything you need."

"Look at the birds in the sky. Aren't they cheerful and happy? They don't work all the time, and yet God takes care of them! Look at the wildflowers. They don't worry about clothes, yet even Solomon didn't look as fine and colorful as they do! God takes care of everything that grows, even if it only lives for a day. If he does that for the birds and the flowers, he will certainly do more for his people."

God Showers His Blessings

Matthew 5:1-12

Jesus went up to the side of the mountain where all the people had gathered to hear him speak.

"My friends," Jesus said, "God blesses those who look to him for help. They belong to the kingdom of heaven! God blesses those who feel sad and hopeless. He will comfort them! God blesses those who are humble. They belong to God! God blesses those who obey him. They will

be given what they ask for! God blesses those who are forgiving and show mercy to others. They will be treated with forgiveness and mercy! God blesses those whose hearts are pure. They will see him! God blesses those who make peace. They will be called his children! God blesses those who are treated badly for doing what is right. They belong to God's kingdom! Be happy! Feel excited and joyful today! For those who do what is right by God will have a big reward in the kingdom of heaven."

The Salt and Light of the Earth

Matthew 5:13-16

Jesus said to his people, "You are the salt of the earth. What would salt be like if it didn't taste salty? You might as well throw it out and walk over it. You, too, will be useless unless you do as you should. Forgive the people that do you wrong. Love each other. Share what you have with others."

Then Jesus said, "You are the shining light that illuminates the world. No one would light a lamp and put it under a clay pot, would they? All the light would be hidden and of no use to anyone. A lamp is placed on a lamp stand where it can give light to everything in the house. Let your light shine bright. Share your light with others. They will see the good you do, and they will do good themselves."

39

40

Coming Together for Jesus

Matthew 18:15-20

Jesus said, "If someone sins against you, go and speak with that person. But do it just between the two of you. If that person listens, you have won back a child of God. If that person refuses to listen, take along one or two others and speak with that person again. If the person still does not hear what you say, go to the church. I promise you that whenever you pray with others and your hearts are one, my Father in heaven will answer your prayer. And whenever two or three of you come together in my name, I am there with you."

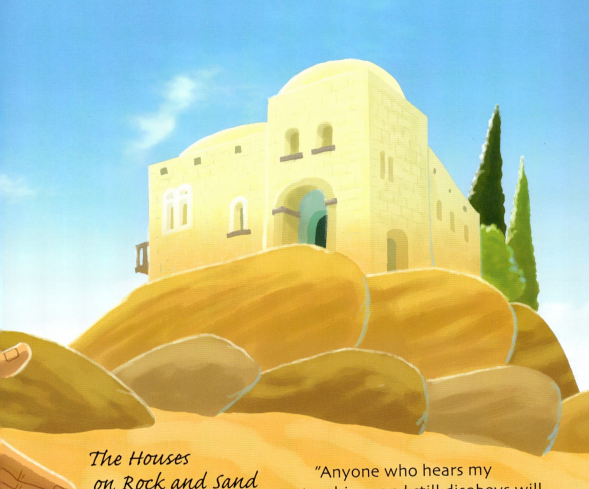

The Houses on Rock and Sand

Matthew 7:24-29

Jesus said, "Anyone who hears and obeys these teachings of mine is like the wise man who built his house on solid rock. Rain poured down, rivers flooded and winds beat against that house. Why did it stay standing? Because it was built on firm ground! Obey my teachings and they will be a solid rock for you. Even when people hurt you or treat you badly, you will stand strong with God."

"Anyone who hears my teachings and still disobeys will be like the foolish man who built a house on sand. Rain poured down, rivers flooded and winds beat against that house. It crumbled right to the ground. The foolish man did not keep my teachings as a solid foundation. But if he had kept my words close to his heart, there would be no storm strong enough to destroy him. God would keep him safe from all harm!"

43

Give Up Everything for God

Mark 10:23-31

Jesus said to his disciples, "It is easier for a camel to go through the eye of a needle than it is for a rich person to get into God's kingdom."

Jesus' disciples were amazed. "But how can anyone ever be saved?" they cried."

"You must give up everything to follow God," Jesus answered. "Anyone who gives up his home or his family or the things he

owns for me will be rewarded."
Peter was glad to hear this. He said, "We left everything to follow you, Jesus!" Jesus turned to him and said, "It is not easy to follow my words. You may be mistreated. You may feel lonely and scared. But in the world to come you will be rewarded with eternal life! Many who are last here on earth will be first in heaven. And many who are first now will later be last."

How to Honor God

Matthew 19:16-22

A rich man came to Jesus and asked, "Teacher, what good things must I do to get into heaven?" Jesus answered, "Only God is truly good. If you want to enter into heaven, obey God's words."

Then the man asked, "Which words should I obey?" Jesus answered, "The commandments: Do not murder. Be faithful in marriage. Do not steal. Do not tell lies. Respect your parents. And love others as you do yourself!"

The man nodded. "Yes, Jesus. I have obeyed all of these rules," he said, "What else should I do?" Jesus replied, "If you want to do more, go beyond simply obeying the rules. Sell the things you own and give to those who do not have anything. Love other people with your whole heart. Forgive the people that hurt you. That way you will truly honor God! Then come and be my follower, and you will be on the right path."

47

The Good Samaritan

Luke 10:25-37

A man stood up and said to Jesus, "The scriptures say to love God with all your heart. They also say to love your neighbor as much as yourself."

"But Jesus," the man asked, "who are my neighbors?"

Jesus told him, "Let me answer your question with a story."

Jesus said, "A traveling man was walking along a deserted road. Robbers came by and attacked him. They stole everything he had and left him lying in a pitiful heap in the middle of the road. Then they ran off. A priest was traveling down the road and came upon the man. He crossed over to the other side and kept on walking. Next, a temple helper came upon the man. He also crossed to the other side of the road and kept on walking. Finally, a Samaritan came by. When he saw the man, he ran to help him. He treated his wounds with oil and put him on his donkey. Then he took him to an inn and told the innkeeper, 'Please care for the man, and I will pay you however much it costs.'"

"Now, which of these three men acted as a neighbor?" Jesus asked.

The man who had asked the question stood up and said, "The Samaritan who showed pity." Jesus answered, "Yes! Now go and do the same."

Lazarus and the Rich Man

Luke 16:19-31

Jesus told a story:

Once there was a rich man. He had expensive clothes, a big house, and all the food he could ask for. One day a beggar named Lazarus came to the man's house asking for the crumbs off of the rich man's table. But the rich man didn't even want to look at Lazarus because he was dirty and sick. The rich man let his dogs sniff Lazarus and lick his wounds. A few days later, both men died. Lazarus went to heaven, but the rich man did not. The rich man cried, "Give me a little water. I am so thirsty!" Abraham in heaven answered,

"When you lived on earth you had everything and yet you did not have pity on Lazarus who had nothing."

The rich man cried out again, "Then warn my brothers who are still alive, so that they don't have to join me here in this horrible place!" Abraham answered, "Moses and all the prophets have already done that. Your brothers should listen to the words that have already been spoken."

"So," Jesus explained, "do not be like the selfish rich man. He realized his lesson only after it was too late. Be like Lazarus—a man of a pure heart. Although he had nothing on earth, he gained the kingdom of heaven."

51

The Farmer's Worthless Harvest

Luke 12:16-21

A young man in the crowd stood up and called to Jesus, "Teacher, tell my brother to be fair and give my share of what our father has left us!"

Jesus answered, "If I did that, it would not help you. What you own will not make your life any better than it is. Think of the farmer who produced a harvest so big that he had to build several new barns just to hold the grain. But the farmer died

52

that very night. What good was all his wealth then?" Then Jesus said to the young man, "Don't be so concerned about what you have and what you don't have. Let God's love be what you hope to possess. Then there will be no end to your wealth!"

God's Heavenly Banquet

Luke 14:16-24

Jesus had been invited to a dinner party by an important Pharisee. Many rich, well-to-do people were there. One among them said, "The greatest blessing of all is to be at the banquet in God's kingdom!" Jesus replied by telling this story:

A man had a banquet full of delicious food prepared. He invited his guests. But the guests kept coming up with reasons why they could not come. One said, "I must tend to the land I've just bought!" Another said, "I'm busy trying out my new oxen." Another said, "I have just gotten married and I cannot come." The master was upset. He told his servant, "Go as fast as you can to every street and alley in town. Bring anyone who is poor or crippled or blind. Let them come to my party!" After the servant did this, there was still room left at the banquet table. So the man said to the servant, "Now go to town and invite everybody you see. But if you see any of the people who rejected my invitation, do not invite them."

Then Jesus turned to the host of the dinner party and said, "Here today you have invited many of your rich friends and neighbors. But I have told you this story to show you that God blesses those who invite the poor, the crippled and the blind. They cannot pay you back. But God will reward you in heaven."

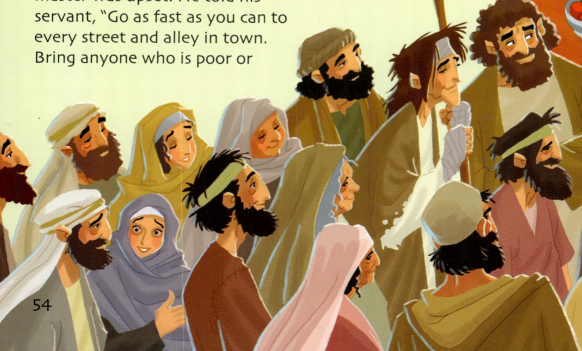

The Ten Bridesmaids

Matthew 25:1-13

Jesus told a story about preparing for God's kingdom:

Once there was going to be a big wedding party. Ten girls took oil lamps to light the darkness while they waited for the groom to come. Five of the girls were wise and brought extra oil. Five of the girls were foolish and did not. The girls waited and waited. Soon they became drowsy and fell asleep. Then someone shouted, "The groom is here! Let's go inside!" The doors of the wedding hall were opened. The

five girls who did not have extra oil cried out, "We are out of oil! Share some with us." But the other five answered, "You must go buy your own." By the time the five girls came back with their oil, the doors had been shut and they could not get in.

"My disciples," Jesus said, "do not be like the five girls who were not prepared. The doors of heaven will not be open to you unless you are ready for God at any moment."

The King and His Official

Matthew 18:21-35

The next story Jesus told was about forgiveness:

One day there lived a king who was collecting money that his officials owed him. An official came in who owed the king fifty million silver coins. But the official had no money. The king gave orders to have him thrown in jail. "Please Your Majesty," the official begged, "have pity on me, and I will pay you back!" The king had a kind heart and decided to let his official go. He even told him that he no longer had to pay his debt.

As the official was walking out feeling happy at his good fortune, he saw a man who owed him one hundred silver coins.

The official grabbed him by the throat and shouted, "Pay back the money you owe me!" The man was frightened. He said, "Have pity on me, and I will pay you back!" But the official showed no pity and had the man thrown in jail. When the king heard about this, he sent for the official. "You owed me money, and I showed mercy on you," said the king. "Why didn't you show mercy on another?" So the king had the official thrown in jail.

Then Jesus said, "My friends, my Father in heaven will show mercy on you, just like the king showed mercy on his official. He expects you to do the same with those around you. Forgive others with all your heart as my Father has forgiven you."

The Three Servants

Luke 19:11-27

Jesus told another story:

There once was a prince who was on his way to a far off land to be crowned king. Before he left, he gave some money to each of his three servants. He told them, "Use this money to make more money. When I return, I will see how you did." After the king returned from his journey, he called in his first servant. The servant exclaimed, "Look! I have earned ten times the amount of money you gave me." The king said, "Wonderful! You have done what I asked. I will give you ten cities to rule over as a reward." Next, the second servant came in. He said, "I have earned five times as much." The king nodded his head in approval. "That is good," he said, "I will give you five cities to rule over."

The third servant came in, looking a little nervous. "I have not made any money," he said. "I was afraid of you, so I just kept the money safe in my handkerchief."

The king was angry. He ordered the money to be given to the man who earned ten times as much. The king's officials were standing nearby and they cried out, "But he already has plenty!" The king replied, "Those who do what I say will be given more. Those who are fearful and do nothing will be given nothing."

"It is the same with the Father in heaven," Jesus explained. "Those who use their lives for his sake shall be given more than they ever dreamed. Those who do not, will be given nothing in return."

The Contemporary Bible Series